GROW UP AND FEEL GREAT!

The Complete Boys' Guide to Growing Up Age 8-12 incl. Body-Care and Self-Esteem Special

Sarah P. Weston

Table of Contents

Introduction.. 5

Changes In Your Body 7

Dealing With New Emotions 12

Expressing Yourself 16

Healthy Diet and Exercise 20

Good Sleep is Key to Health............................ 25

The Importance of Good Hygiene.......................29

Changing Friendships 33

Saying NO to Peer Pressure..............................36

How to Cope with Bullying 40

Finding the Time: School and Studying 48

Finding Your Favourite Hobbies.........................52

Girls and Relationships 55

Understanding girls.. 58

Finding Role Models...61

Learning Your Identity...64

Body care and self-esteem...68

Taking care of your body.. 69

Boosting your self-esteem 71

The "Embarrassing" Stuff 75

Conclusion 78

Disclaimer 80

Introduction

The ages of eight to twelve years old can be a big time of change for any boy. At the age of eight, you are starting to understand the word more clearly than you did when you were younger. You might enjoy new hobbies and start to be learning about yourself.

By the time you reach the age of twelve, your body and your mind will have changed and grown a lot. You will be able to express your thoughts more easily and you will probably have a lot of questions about the world. You might be starting to wonder where you fit into society and what other people think about you.

During this time, as your brain and body are changing, you are likely to become more aware of things like your body image and what you look like to yourself, in the mirror, and others including your friends and girls.

Building your self-esteem is very important during these years because it can be a time when you can feel sad or bad about yourself. Making sure that you feel good about yourself now and that you respect your body and know all your good qualities can also make sure that you will feel good about yourself as you grow up.

Over the next few years, you will start to change from being a boy into becoming a man. It might be hard to think about it now, but within the next ten years you will *become* a man. You will grow, have a deeper voice, be stronger and be able to do things that you cannot even imagine right now.

In this book, we are going to look at some of the main changes that will happen to your body and your mind over the four years between the ages of eight and twelve, before you become a teenager. We will explore the different ways that you can cope with hard times and challenges in the next few years.

You will also learn some tools from this book that will help you to feel good about yourself. You can use these now but also in the future, during your teenage years and after that too. That means that you can grow up and feel great!

Changes In Your Body

When you reach the age of 10 or 11 or sometimes a little older, you will start to go through a stage of your life called "puberty." This stage will last for most of your teens and it is the time of your life when you will change the most.

It can be scary when you start puberty because you will notice lots of things that are different with your body. At first, you might not understand what is happening, so here are some of the signs that you might see when puberty begins:

- ✪ You start to grow pubic hair – hair that is in the area between your legs – and it can become darker, curlier and thicker.

- ✪ You might begin to sweat more and more easily than you used to when you were younger.

- ✪ Your penis and testicles start to grow and this area becomes darker.

- ✪ Your breasts can become bigger for a while – *yes*, boys also have breasts. This usually only lasts for a little while and it doesn't mean that you have "man boobs" or "moobs."

✪ You might start to experience "wet dreams." This is where a substance called semen comes out of your penis when you are sleeping.

✪ Your voice will start to break – it will sound deeper sometimes at first but then it might sound high and squeaky. Over time it will smooth out and sound deeper more of the time.

✪ You start to get spots on your face. This is known as acne. It can be worse for some boys than others. Serious acne can sometimes be treated by a doctor.

✪ You will grow a lot taller which is known as having a "growth spurt." This can happen at any time from the age of 12 until around 16 or 17. For most boys, you will grow by around 8 cm a year throughout puberty.

✪ You will notice that your arms, legs, tummy and chest start to become more muscular.

Puberty can be a scary time in your time because there are a lot of changes happening at the same time. Your body is changing very fast. But you are not alone. Your friends will also go through the exact same thing as you are going through. They might also have the same fears that you have.

This can be a time when you feel unsure about what is happening to you. It is normal to be confused. So, it is really important that you find someone that you can talk to about how you feel. Some boys feel comfortable talking to a friend their own age. Other boys want to talk to an adult, like your dad or an uncle. Older brothers can also be good for getting support because they have been through the same thing really recently.

It can be weird and awkward for you if you go through these changes before your friends do. You might feel like you are the "odd one out" and that you are strange compared to everyone else. Remember that your friends and all the other boys you know will also go through the same things sooner or later.

As your body changes, you might notice there are things that you are happy about and things that you are not happy about. You might feel insecure – which means that you do not feel good enough about your body or parts of your body.

Having a good body image is really important for feeling confident. When you feel good about the way you look you accept your body and take good care of it. You will also feel proud of your body and all the amazing things that it can do.

When your body changes, especially really fast, this can affect the way that you feel about yourself. If you have been shy as a younger boy or even if you were always confident, the changes in your body can mean that you don't feel so confident anymore.

So, how can you feel better about yourself when you start to feel bad or sad about the way that you look?

Here are some top tips for making yourself feel better:

✪ **Look for the good things about your body** – Concentrate on the things that you do like and not the stuff that you are not happy about. The more time you spend thinking about the good things, the more they will be at the front of your mind rather than the bad.

✪ **Try to be more aware of your body** – Think of the amazing things that your body can do. There are all kinds of different systems and organs in your body and you have millions of cells in your body. It is constantly growing and changing, and take notice of that in a positive way instead of seeing it as a bad thing.

✪ **Give your body what it needs** – A healthy body feels good. So, when you are feeling bad about yourself, play some sports or exercise or eat some food that is healthy but tastes nice.

✪ **Do not compare yourself with other people** – It can be really easy to want to look at other boys and think: "I wish I looked like him." This can make you feel really bad about yourself and make your self-esteem low. It is better to look at your own good points instead of thinking about other people's.

✪ **Make the best of yourself** – If you are feeling bad about the way you look, you can probably make some small changes that will be easy to do but will make a big difference. Change your hair or get some new clothes that you like. This can make you feel a lot better about your looks.

Dealing With New Emotions

As we talked about in the last chapter, puberty can bring changes to your body and make it look and feel different than it used to be. As you get older, you can also start to feel and experience new emotions too. Emotions are the way that you feel – such as happy, sad, angry or worried. You might also start to feel more self-conscious around other people too. Again, this is normal and it is something that everyone goes through – both boys and girls.

As you are heading toward puberty, it is normal to experience "mood swings." This is because you have something in your body called *hormones*. These are substances that can make you feel a certain way when there are more or less of them in your body. Different organs in your body produce these hormones and as you get older, you start to produce more of them.

One of the most important hormones for boys and men is called *testosterone*. When you reach puberty, your body makes more testosterone than it did when you were younger. This is one of the reasons that your body goes through all the changes, like growing hair and your voice breaking. But testosterone can also affect the way that you feel too.

As you start to make more of this hormone in your body, it can affect your mood. Sometimes, it can make you feel angry, careless or sad. At your age, your body is learning how to cope with having more testosterone. It is a new experience for your body and your brain so it will take time to get used to it.

For example, it is like when you take up a new hobby. Do you remember the first time that you tried to play your favourite sport? You might not have been very good at it to start with. You might even have missed kicking or hitting the ball the very first few times. As you played that sport more often, you got better at it. You learned how to do it without even thinking about it and it became a lot easier to you.

Well, your body is learning how to cope with all these new hormones in the same way that you learned how to play that sport. It takes time and practice for your body to be able to handle it. For this reason, at the start of your journey through puberty, you can often experience lots of changes in your mood and feel overwhelmed by your emotions sometimes.

So, what are some good ways to learn how to cope with these new changes in your feelings?

- ✪ **Do not keep your feelings bottled up** – Talking is a good way to understand how you are feeling when you have lots of confusing new emotions in your head. You can talk to lots of different people and they will give you different but helpful advice. Sometimes, it can be good to talk to a friend but other times you might need to talk to an adult, like one of your parents.

- ✪ **Find things to do that you enjoy** – When you are finding your new feelings really hard to deal with, it can be good for you to do a hobby or sport that you really find fun. This can take your mind off your worries and pass the time until the strange emotions stop upsetting you.

- ✪ **Keep on top of things** – It can be really easy to get worried about a lot of things. For example, if you are just starting high school, this is a new experience for you and it will cause you to have a lot of new feelings. So, try and stay organised so that you do not get behind with any of your schoolwork or chores.

- ✪ **Do not be too hard on yourself** – If it feels strange to have all these new feelings and thoughts in your head, do not be hard on yourself because of that. It is normal and natural and you need to know that every boy (and every girl) is going through this same thing at your age. So, if you get upset, angry or stressed out, try and be caring towards yourself and realise that your new feelings and emotions will eventually start to settle down.

Expressing Yourself

For many boys, it can sometimes be difficult to talk about the way you're feeling. You might have grown up with the outside influences of being told that *men do not talk about their feelings.* It is important to understand that being a boy or a girl does not stop you from having feelings and it should not stop you from talking about the way you feel.

Everyone feels down at times. Some days, you will wake up and you will feel sad or angry. If you keep those feelings inside, instead of talking about them with the people around you, it can make you feel worse. Over time, the feelings can gradually build up until you notice that they start to come out when you don't expect it.

Talking to other people has a lot of benefits. There is a saying that: "a problem shared is a problem halved." This means that when you talk to someone about your problems, stresses and worries, the problem seems less bad because they share the burden of it. Another benefit of talking to someone about your problems is that you can also get some really great advice from other people.

Some boys find it hard to talk to other people about what they are going through because they feel embarrassed about talking. For example, if you are having worries about your body image, you might not want to talk to someone about it because the media and other people in society sometimes show the image that boys should not talk about their problems. Over the past few years, many men and boys have shown that talking is really important. Even some of the British Royal family have talked about the kinds of worries that they have. Lots of male sports stars and celebrities are also talking more about the things that affect them badly and saying how much it helps them to express themselves.

So, when you talk to a friend or relative about the problems you have, you will feel much better afterward too.

So, who can you talk to?

It is always a good idea to talk to your mum or dad but as you get older, you might be shy to talk to them about private things. For example, as you notice changes in your body, you may feel embarrassed to speak with your parents about this. In this case, there are other people you can also talk to. If you have a trusted relative, like an uncle or a family friend who can talk to you, they will probably want to listen and help with your problems. Teachers at your school or sports coaches that you can trust are a good option too. Teachers and coaches are used to being around boys of your age and they probably went through similar issues and feelings when they were younger too.

Friends are also a great choice for talking. One of the good things about talking to your friends about things that bother you is that they are probably experiencing the same or similar worries right now. Their bodies and minds are changing too so they will be able to make you feel less alone in what you are going through right now.

If you do not feel comfortable talking to anyone that you know, one other option is to call a helpline that is meant for kids. This will give you the chance to talk to a stranger who will not judge you and will listen to your problems. They will have a lot of experience in dealing with the kinds of things that you want to talk about and can give you really good and practical advice to help you feel better or make changes that will improve things for you.

No matter whom you talk to, the main thing is that you express yourself. Sometimes, you don't even have to express yourself out loud to another person. One really helpful tip to make you feel better and let you express yourself without having to talk to someone else is to write your thoughts and feelings down in a journal.

Keeping a daily journal can also be really good because when you are feeling down, you can look back through your diary to find that there have been times before when you have felt like this but it always got better. So, you will then know that it will get better again. That is an important thing to remember when you are feeling sad- things *do* get better in time.

Healthy Diet and Exercise

Eating a healthy diet and exercising is very important for people of all ages. But, if you start to eat healthy food now and do lots of sports or exercise, it will also be good for you when you get older too.

Right now, you might not like the idea of "healthy" food. Lots of boys think that healthy means just a plate of vegetables and it is very bland. But you can actually learn to cook when you are young and ask your mum and dad to teach you. This can be really helpful when you get older because if you live on your own you will be able to feed yourself and impress your friends and girlfriends.

So, you might be curious how you can make healthy food more interesting. Well, firstly, think of your favourite junk foods – fish and chips, burger and fries, pizza? You can learn how to make healthier versions of all of these and they will be really tasty.

For example, if you are a big fan of fish and chips, you can ask your mum and dad or your guardian to make you a version that does not have lots of oil in it. So, they can bake the fish rather than frying it. Instead of chips that are made with potatoes, they can use sweet potatoes as these are much healthier and they count as one of the five fruits and veggies that you are supposed to eat every day to keep your body healthy.

Another favourite food of boys is burger and fries. Against, you can make this much healthier and even tastier by making a homemade version. You can cook with your mum and dad. Instead of getting takeaway versions, it is often better and healthier to prepare meals at home because you know what kinds of foods are going into the dish. Also, they don't have any nasty chemicals in them which can sometimes be bad for you.

When it comes to snacks, many boys love their chocolate, crisps and other types of sweets. There is nothing wrong with eating these foods but it is a good idea to make sure that you do not eat too much. Eating too many sweets can make your teeth decay and make you gain weight too. They can also make you feel like you have too much energy and you can become restless and feel like you don't know what to do with yourself. This is also a good reason for avoiding energy drinks as they have a lot of bad chemicals in them and can make you feel hyperactive.

When you feel like snacking, there are some healthier types of snacks. Kale chips are really tasty and they are a healthy replacement for crisps. Frozen grapes, strawberries or blueberries can be a delicious alternative to sweets. Remember that sometimes it can take time for your mind to change when you try a new type of food. At first, you might think that you don't like it so try different fruits a few times before you make up your mind.

Overall, a balanced diet with all types of food groups is the healthiest way to live. Your diet should have vitamins and minerals – which are nutrients that keep your body healthy and well. You should also eat protein, fat and carbohydrates too. It is also important to make sure that you eat enough calories every day but that you do not eat too many because this can make you gain weight.

A calorie is a measure of how much energy is in a piece of food. For most boys between eight and twelve years old, you should be eating between 1,600 and 2,200 calories per day but you might need to eat more or less than this if you are very active or if do not do a lot of exercises. So, if you play a lot of sports, you might need more calories than a boy who is also your age but does very little exercise. For foods that are in jars, packets or tins, you can find the number of calories in your foo on the back of the packaging.

Calories can be important if you are trying to lose weight. You should only lose weight if you have been told by a doctor or nurse that you need to do this. When you get older, you will use up a lot more calories than you do now, especially when you become a teenager. Some teenage boys use up to 3,000 calories every day so they will need more food than other people.

You take calories in when you eat but you use those calories up when you exercise. In fact, you are always using calories, even when you sleep. They are fuel just like when your parents put petrol or diesel into your family car. Unlike a car, you are using calories even when you are at rest. However, when you are sitting down and watching television or sleeping you will only burn around one calorie every minute. This is a good reason not to spend too much time sitting down and playing video games or watching TV. Instead, it is really good for you to get active instead.

Exercise is a very good way to stay healthy and it's also great for having fun with your friends. Sometimes, it can be a good way to relax too. If you are part of a team, you can meet new people and make new friends. Exercise has a lot of benefits. You will notice, especially at this time of your life, that you start to build and tone your muscle. As you now have new hormones (like testosterone) in your body and you are on your journey toward becoming a man, it will be easier for your muscle to develop than it used to be.

When you exercise, you are keeping fit, burning calories, strengthening your muscles and keeping your organs (such as your heart and lungs) very healthy. You can also notice that your mood feels lighter when you exercise. As you move into puberty, it is good to have natural ways to make yourself feel happier because you will experience some mood swings. This is natural but it can be frustrating and annoying for you and for the people who are around you, such as your family and friends.

There are lots of different types of exercise that you can enjoy. Here are a few different examples of some sports and activities that you take part in:

- ✪ Walking – this is one of the easiest types of exercise to do and it will not cost anything as your parents will not have to pay a fee for you to join a club. You can try and get your whole family involved and ask them to go out with you for an evening or weekend walk.

- ✪ Running – like walking, this type of exercise is really easy to do and you can do it as often as you want on your own or with other people. If you are trying to lose weight or train to get fit, running is a really good type of exercise and it is beneficial for your heart.

- ✪ Football – many boys love football and it is a fun activity to play with your mates or with new people. You can play with friends on your local field or, if you want to take it more seriously, you can join a club or a team.

- ✪ Cycling – in the UK, cycling has become a lot more popular since many British professional cyclists have been very successful at major sports events such as the Olympic Games and the Tour de France (one of the world's major cycling competitions.) You can take your cycle to the park and you will get a really good workout. There are also a lot of kids cycling clubs that will help you to train and take your cycling to another level.

✪ Martial arts – there are many different types of martial arts such as karate, judo and taekwondo. Martial arts can keep you in really good shape but they are also good because they help you to learn how to defend yourself as well. They can also teach you things like self-discipline, motivation and organisational skills.

✪ Tennis, golf, badminton and other sports – there are so many different sports that you can play and now is a great time to try out a different range of sports. From basketball to volleyball to cricket to rugby, you will be able to find a favourite type of exercise and activity. If you do not enjoy one sport, then move on and try another. It might take some time to find the right one for you but do not give up. Even if you do not enjoy your gym classes at school, there might be some sports that you have not even thought of but you would love.

In the end, doing exercise of any type can really help you to be healthy and feel good. It can really make your body look great which will make you feel better if you have some body issues and you have insecurities that are making you feel bad right now.

Good Sleep is Key to Health

A healthy diet and doing lots of exercises is really important for being healthy but you will also find that one of the most important parts of being kind to your body and your mind is getting lots of good sleep.

There are different kinds of sleep, such as lighter and deeper sleep but the main thing for having a healthy body is to make sure that you are getting enough sleep every night. It is good to have a bedtime and stick to it so that you get into a good routine. Try to avoid things that can make you sleep badly or send you to sleep late like video games.

Between the ages of eight and twelve years old you will need between ten and eleven hours of sleep every night. So, if you have to be up for 7 am, this means that you should be in bed by 8 pm or 9 pm the night before. Getting enough sleep is very important for your body to feel fresh and for your mind to feel awake. If you have ever stayed up late on a school night, you will know how difficult it was to concentrate in your classes the next day.

Some of the main benefits of good sleep are:

✪ You will get ill less often

✪ You will be less likely to put on weight

✪ You will feel happier and more positive

✪ You will worry less and not feel stressed as much or as often

✪ Your thoughts will be clearer and more focused so you can do better in school

✪ You are more likely to get along with people better

Of course, sometimes, especially if you have some things on your mind, it is not always easy to fall asleep. If you have a big test the next day, it can be really hard to sleep because you will be thinking about it a lot and worrying so much that you cannot stop your thoughts.

Luckily, if you have trouble falling asleep sometimes, there are some ways that you can change this.

- ✪ Listen to relaxing music that is very calming and will help you drift off to sleep.

- ✪ Make sure your bedroom curtains are fully closed and that your room is dark. Also, if you are feeling too hot or too cold, it can be hard to sleep so you might need to open a window or ask your parents to turn on the heating.

- ✪ Take a warm bath before you go to bed as that can make you feel really sleepy.

- ✪ Do not do anything before bed that makes you mind feel really active like lots of studying or playing video games.

- ✪ Try to do a lot of different activities during the daytime so that you feel really tired when it is time for bed.

- ✪ Drink a cup of chamomile tea as this is very calming and it is suitable for children of all ages.

Getting lots of sleep can be very good for you. It is really important and you will notice that you feel like you have a lot more energy when you have slept well. Another benefit of a good night's sleep is that when you are asleep, you have dreams. Dreams are really important because they are the way that your brain sorts through all the things that you have learned that day. Dreams also help your mind to calm any worries that you might have.

The Importance of Good Hygiene

Hygiene is very important at all ages but as you take responsibility for your own hygiene, it is important to know that you need to remove the germs from your body. There are germs on your skin and in places like your mouth, so it is important to wash yourself and brush your teeth every day.

As your body goes through puberty, you will notice that you have more hair on your body and that you sweat more. This means that you will start to smell more easily. It is not a nice thought but you can help to prevent yourself from smelling by taking regular showers or baths.

You can buy nice smelling products that can also help you to smell good if you use them when you bathe or shower. At first, it might seem like these kinds of products are "girly" but they are really just meant to keep you smelling fresh. It is nice when anyone smells good and should not just be something for girls.

Another important part of your daily hygiene is to make sure that you brush your teeth every day. It is a good idea to brush your teeth two to three times every day, especially if you eat sweet foods with lots of sugar in them or if you drink fizzy soda drinks or energy drinks. If you do not brush your teeth enough, you can start to get tooth decay, when your teeth rot. You can also end up with bleeding gums, bad breath and pain. If you get bad teeth, this can make you feel really bad about your looks. So, taking care of your teeth stops this from happening in the first place.

One of the big signs of puberty, and probably one of the most annoying, is when you start to get acne. Acne is another word for spots or pimples and you can get them anywhere on your body or face. When they are on your face, you might feel that you look bad or that other people are looking at you. Mostly, people understand that you are going through a time of change in your life and acne affects almost everybody at some point.

Acne is usually caused by hormones and so it cannot be prevented or cured by good hygiene. It is not caused by bad hygiene either. However, washing your face with a medicated facewash every day can help to keep your skin clean and stop too many germs from being on your skin. You can also help to prevent infections on your skin or stop your acne from becoming infected, which can be very painful, if you have good skin hygiene.

At this time of your life, you should be sure to wash your hair regularly, especially if it is longer. Unwashed hair can have a nasty smell and it can look greasy and not nice. To make it easier for you, you can buy all-in-one hair and body washes. This means that you can use the same liquid soap to wash your hair and body. So, you can save time and energy by washing both your body and your hair when you have a shower.

As you get older, probably when you reach your teens, you will need to start shaving too. As you have noticed, you are growing more hair on your body and you will also start to grow hair on the parts of your face such as your upper lip and your chin. When you first start to grow hair on your face, it will be a little fuzzy and it will not be long enough to grow a proper beard. However, that can be a good time to learn how to shave. Ask your dad or another trusted older male relative to show you how to shave properly so that you do not cut yourself.

Overall, good hygiene is really important for keeping yourself clean, making sure that you smell good, preventing infections on your skin and making people like you more. The truth is that people, both adults and other children, will respect you more if you are clean and tidy. A good hygiene routine can be helpful through your whole life so now is a really great time to get into good habits. If you are struggling or you have questions, your parents can talk you through the things that you need to do every day and how to do them.

Changing Friendships

In your life you may have had the same groups of friends since you were little or you might have had lots of different groups of friends. As you move from primary school toward high school, it is natural that you will notice changes in your group of friends. Every boy goes through this because you are growing up and changing and your friends are changing too.

Of course, it can make you feel sad if you start to notice that you are not as close to your old friends as you used to be or if they drift away from you and don't want to spend as much time around you as they used to. It can also hurt if your closest friends find new friends.

For example, you might have a best friend that you have been close to since you were in reception class. You have been through everything together, learning to ride your bikes together, playing your first game of football together, even going on holiday with each other's families.

But *now* things have changed. Your friend doesn't want to spend time with you as much as he used to. He's started doing new hobbies and he's found other friends. How do you feel? Sad? Angry? Hurt? All these feelings are normal but they might feel confusing to you at first because you are not used to them. Everything feels like it is changing so fast and you want things to go back to the way they used to be.

It can be hard to feel great when you feel like the changes in your life are not a good thing. You might feel lonely and want to be back in a safer time when you felt that you had lots of friends around you. You may ever feel slightly resentful about the changes. However, it is just a part of life. As you grow up, you will experience many different kinds of changes and these are good for helping you grow and learn as you move forward.

This can also happen if you have a best friend who is a girl. Girls change, just like boys change and sometimes, when girls start to get a little older, they don't want to hang out with boys anymore. They want to spend their time with other friends who are girls. This can make you feel like you have lost your friend or that you are not good enough but you should always remember that is *not* true. This is just a part of growing up and at your age, you might also start to notice that girls and boys are different. Right now, you might not even like girls very much but for most boys, that will change as you get older.

Saying NO to Peer Pressure

As you get older, especially when you start high school, you will find that new pressures are around that you have not noticed in the past. For example, you may find that other people in your class are doing harmful things like drinking or smoking.

Drinking and smoking can really have a bad effect on your body and they can cause lots of long-term side effects that do not feel nice. If you want to keep your body cared for and in the best sort of shape, then it is a very good idea to steer clear of anything that can hurt you.

It is normal to be curious about new experiences but you should also be aware of how harmful these things can be to you. Drinking and smoking can hurt your body and make you feel very ill. It can also really upset the people that love you, like your parents and siblings to know that you have tried alcohol or cigarettes.

Of course, it can be hard to say no when you are out with your friends and they are trying to pressurise you to try drinking or smoking. So, it is important to know how to say *no* and stick to it. Remember that it doesn't make you "uncool" if you don't drink or smoke. When you get older, people will actually have more respect for a man who knows his own mind and can say no. It makes you a leader instead of a follower.

If you say no and your friends say something like: "Why don't you just try it once?" then you might find it hard to say no again. But here are some facts about drinking, smoking and other things that people might try and pressure you to do:

Drinking:

- ✪ Alcohol, like beer, wine and cider can cause cancer, especially when you are younger.

- ✪ It can make you feel sad all the time and make you feel angry more easily.

- ✪ It can harm your heart and other organs, like your liver and your brain.

- ✪ People tend to do silly things when they drink alcohol – such as climbing up onto high walls and falling off or hitting people

- ✪ Committing crimes is more likely if you drink alcohol and this can mean that you get into trouble with the police.

- ✪ You might not be able to keep up with your schoolwork because you will not be able to concentrate in class if you feel ill or tired from drinking. It can also make you more likely to get kicked out of school.

Smoking:

- ✪ Smoking can cause cancer and other illnesses.

- ✪ It can make you smell bad and if your clothes and hair are stinky, other people will not want to be around you.

- ✪ It can make your teeth turn yellow or brown even if you brush them regularly.

- ✪ It is very expensive and will use up all the money from your allowance.

Drugs:

- ✪ Drugs can kill you. Every year, hundreds of young people die from drugs.

- ✪ They can harm your body and your brain.

- ✪ They can affect your schoolwork.

- ✪ People who take drugs can commit crimes or do things that hurt themselves or other people.

So, if your friends try and make you try any of these things or other bad things, you can see why it is a good idea to always say no. If your friends say they will not be friends with you anymore if you don't try these friends, remember that there are always other friends out there who will respect your choices and will not try to make you do these things. *Real friends* do not pressure you into doing stuff that you don't want to do.

When you find yourself under peer pressure to do something, you could feel that people will not think that you are cool or that people will laugh at you or tease you if you do not do what they suggest. It is much worse for your body to suffer from long-term harm than it is to deal with some teasing.

How to Cope with Bullying

One of the hardest things to deal with in life is being bullied. The truth is that many boys (and girls too) get bullied at some time in their lives. Even adults can also be bullied when they go to work. So, it is important to know that being bullied is nothing to be ashamed of. In fact, it is the bullies that should be ashamed of themselves and what they do.

Still, when you are being bullied, it can make you feel really bad. You might feel sad and that nobody in the world cares about you. You can also feel really angry at the bully and the world too. Your self-esteem can be hurt and you might feel like it is your fault – even though it is never your fault.

The first thing to know is that bullies tend to be very scared themselves. They feel like they do not have any power so they might bully a boy who is younger than they are or smaller than they are so that they can feel bigger and better about themselves. This can be really hard to understand because it is strange and upsetting that some people can be so mean.

But *it is never your fault.*

These days, bullying can happen in a lot of different places. In the olden days, most bullies bullied people at school or when they saw people at the park or other places. Now, bullies can bully people online too. As you get older now and start to use the internet and social media more, it is really important to know that bullies can use social media, text messages and phone calls to bully people.

Here is a story about a young boy who was bullied and you may have already heard similar stories in your life:

Max was a young boy of twelve years old. He had always been a happy boy with lots of friends. He loved to play football and go to the park with his mum, dad and sister and sometimes he would hang out with his friends. He was good in school and always got good marks on his tests.

One day, he was in his P.E class and there was another boy, called Louis, who was in the same class. Max had known Louis for a long time but they had never been friends because Louis always seemed kind of mean. That day, in class, they were playing a game of football and Max was made to be one of the team captains and he had to pick all the members of the teams. He didn't like Louis so he didn't pick him for the team.

The boys and girls all played the game of football and Max's team won. Max scored the winning goal, putting the winner past Louis who was the goalkeeper for the other team. At the time, Louis seemed upset but he was very quiet and did not say anything.

That night, Max went home and ate dinner with his family and he told his parents and his sister all about his day and how he had won a game of football at school. His mum and dad were very proud of him. He asked them if he could use the computer to check his social media account and they agreed. He had only had a social media account for a few months, since he turned twelve but it made him feel very grown up and it meant that he could keep in touch with his friends.

When he went online, he noticed that he had a message on his account so he opened it excitedly. But when he saw it, he froze. The message was from Louis and it was very mean. It called him a lot of horrible names and Louis said that he was going to "get him" because Max had embarrassed him during their game of football.

Max was upset but he thought that things would be fine by the next day and that Louis must have been hurt and sad but he would get over it. However, Louis didn't get over it. Over the next few days, he would bump Max's shoulder every time that he saw him in the hallways in school.

When the weekend came, Max was very glad and relieved. He was happy that he could finally relax and that he wouldn't have to see Louis for a while. That weekend, Max's mum and dad took him and his sister to the zoo. They saw all the animals and had a great time. They also took a lot of pictures. When they got home, Max decided to post some of their pictures on his social media account before he went to bed.

The next morning, Max woke up and checked his account to see if anyone had liked his pictures or commented on them. He was very upset when he saw that Louis had left lots of mean comments on every picture, calling him a "loser" and "ugly." Max wanted to cry and he felt very angry at knowing that Louis felt that way. For the rest of the weekend, he hid away in his room.

Over the next few weeks and months, Louis got worse. He would be horrible to Max at school and he would say many mean things to him on social media. Louis made Max feel really bad about himself. Max started to believe all the things Louis was saying, even though he had never thought that those things were true before.

Instead of going out with his family and friends, Max hid away in his room, feeling very down and sad. He didn't spend as much time with his friends in school either. He could concentrate on his schoolwork and his marks started to get worse. Some of his teachers noticed that his work was not as good as it used to be, so they asked him about it but Max told them that everything was fine. He didn't want to tell them the truth because he was embarrassed about being bullied, he thought it was his fault and he thought that it would get even worse if he snitched on Louis.

One day, Max's uncle came to town to visit. He lived a little while away so he didn't come to visit the family very often. But as soon as he arrived, his uncle noticed that there was something wrong with Max. When he asked Max about it, Max still didn't want to say anything but his uncle promised him that he could trust him and tell him anything. Even though Max was still a little scared, to tell the truth, he finally told his uncle what was going on. His uncle was shocked and upset that Max had been going through that alone. He wanted Max to talk to his parents. Eventually, Max agreed.

That day, Max told his mum and dad everything that had happened and they were really sad that their boy had gone through all of this, especially as Louis had been able to affect him everywhere, from when they were in school to even when Max was at home, as a lot of the bullying was online. They went to see Max's teachers and the teachers took action. They told Louis that he would face a lot of bad *things, like being kicked out of school, if he kept on acting that way. Louis agreed he wouldn't do it anymore.*

It took a long time for Max to recover and he felt like he had to build his self-esteem and confidence again. He talked to the school counsellor and she helped him to realise that it was not his fault that he had been bullied. She also helped him to realise all the good qualities that he had and that he was not ugly or stupid or any of the other things Louis had said about him.

Eventually, Max felt stronger and happier and he grew up to be a very clever boy who had lots of friends. But he always remembered how easy it was to lose confidence and he understood the importance of sharing his problems with other people and getting help when he needed it, even when it was hard.

As you can see from this story, it is very easy for a bully to affect someone and it can be difficult to deal with a bully on your own. When someone is bullied, they can lose their confidence and feel scared, especially when the bully can even reach them in their own home. If you are going through a situation like Max has gone through, you can also get through it, just like Max did. Even then it seems hard and dark, remember that the night always turns into day again and that there are ways to stop the bullying and make yourself feel better.

If you have been bullied or you are going through something like that right now, there are some ways that you can help yourself and stop the bully from getting to you. These tips can help you to tackle the bullying:

✪ **Do not listen to the bully** – Bullying can happen in person or on your phone or by social media sites on the internet but it is important to try not to get into a conversation with the bully or listen to what they say. If they come to you and talk to you, do not even answer them. If they send you a message online or on your phone, delete it and do not even read it.

✪ **Do not get angry** – It can be difficult not to get angry when all you want to do is to yell and shout at the bully. When they are saying mean things, it is easy to let your temper get out of control and that is exactly what the bully is trying to do. They want to see a reaction from you and they want to see you angry and upset because they are trying to be as mean as they possibly can be. However, if you do not react with anger or sadness, then they have failed and this will make them feel bad instead of making you feel bad.

✪ **Seek support from your friends** – Friends can give you protection from bullies if you talk to them. Good friends will be people that you can rely on and will take your side to help you if your bully is around. This can make you feel like you are not alone when you are dealing with the bully. When you find that your bully targets you online, you can talk to a sibling who may be able to support you or offer you some good advice.

✪ **Talk to a parent, guardian or teacher** – One of the best ways to help stop the bully from hurting you can be to turn to a parent, a guardian or one of your teachers. At first, it might be scary to think of telling someone what is going on and sometimes it might seem even scarier than the bullying. It can be hard and you might think that telling someone will make it even worse sometimes the only way to stop the bully is to talk to an adult. They will have more power than the bully so they can take good steps to prevent the bully from behaving the way they have been in the past.

✪ **Rebuild your self-esteem and your confidence** – Bullying can often take away a lot of your self-confidence. It can bring up a lot of bad feelings inside you. You might feel worthless, stupid and ugly, even though you are not. It can take some work to make yourself feel better again. It might take some time before you recover from what you have been through with the bullying experience. In some cases, if you have been through an experience that has caused a lot of traumas, you might need to talk to a counsellor or therapist. Your parents will be able to spend some time with you, talking through all the various options.

Anyone can be a victim of bullying and that does not mean that there is something wrong with you. Lots of famous and successful people have talked about how they were bullied when they were kids. As long as you have people around to support you, like your family, friends or teachers, then you have the support that you need to stop the bully.

The most important thing is that you are not afraid to talk about what you are going through. When you stay silent, then a bully wins. They want you to keep quiet so they can keep upsetting you. But if you speak out and tell other people, then the bully loses and they have no more power. Remember that a bully wants to harm your confidence and self-esteem. They want to make you feel ugly and worthless. They want to hurt you by telling you horrible things that are not true.

Speak out and do not let them win.

Finding the Time:
School and Studying

As a young boy who is in the middle of your development between childhood and your teenage years, one of the biggest changes that will happen in your educational and social life is going from primary school to high school.

School can bring a lot of stress with it. You are trying to get good marks in your schoolwork, joining extracurricular clubs and activities, dealing with your changing body and other side effects of puberty like a breaking voice and making new friends.

Organising your time can be really important when you go to school so that you have enough time to spend doing all the things you need. If you do not have the time, then the important things that you need to do to keep your body and mind healthy can end up being left behind. It can be easier said than done, of course. When you have a lot of homework at night and you have to keep up with chores at home too, you might find that you do not have the time to do exercise or to spend time eating dinner with your family.

A great tip to make sure that you have the time to do all the things you need to do is to make a plan for each day so that you know what you are doing. Of course, when you want to keep your body healthy, you should always ensure that you make some time in your timetable for exercise.

Another problem that you might notice when it comes to your diet at high school is that you are tempted to snack more during your break times and lunchtimes. If you have put in some hard work to make your diet healthier, this can be bad for your diet and make you go back to feeling bad about your body and yourself if you put on some weight. Also, even when you have a well-organised timetable, you might notice that you are very tired after you finish school and not feel like exercising.

At this point, it is a good idea to try and find a way around these problems. For example, can you take healthy snacks with you to school so that you do not snack on chocolate and crisps when you have a break? Can you spend time at the weekends doing some exercise if you do not have the time on a school night?

Of course, the main reason that you go to school is to study and that is what we are going to focus on now. Getting good marks on your tests, projects and essays can be a really big factor in your level of self-esteem. If you fail a test, it can make you feel sad and disappointed in yourself. If you do really well on a test or project, it can make you feel good about yourself and have a lot of confidence in your abilities. For this reason, finding time to study is very important.

One of the biggest things that stops boys from studying and doing their homework can be noise and distractions at home. If you have siblings and they are always around and very noisy or if you share a room, it can be really tough to get some time alone to concentrate on studying and doing your homework.

If this is the case for you, there are some ways around it. Firstly, it is a good idea to make sure that your family is aware of your problem. Your brothers or sisters might not realise that they are distracting you and they could be very upset to know that they are badly affecting you. However, if the situation cannot be changed, then you should try and find a quiet place where you can study. Most towns and cities have a local library where you can spend some time alone in a quiet room with the chance to do all of your work. This can help you to get good marks and feel really great about yourself!

When you are at school, there are many different ways that you can find to boost your self-esteem. Joining clubs and being good at lots of different activities is a fantastic way of doing this. Have a look at the different societies, clubs and activities that your school offers and you might be able to find something that makes you want to join. Remember that doing something you enjoy and you are good at is the perfect way to increase your self-esteem. So, even if you get bad marks on a test, if you do well at chess club it can make up for it.

Finding Your Favourite Hobbies

As you move from childhood into your preteen or "tween" years, you'll be changing a lot. You will notice that you start to like new things and find new hobbies. Sometimes, it can be hard to find time to fit in everything that you want to do into your day or week. But hobbies are very important because, when you are growing up, they can be important to help you develop well and feel really good about yourself.

If you have ever heard adults talking about how "well-rounded" someone is, this means that they have a lot of skills in a lot of different areas. So, someone might be very clever but they might also be really great at playing football and good at drawing and painting too.

When you are working on improving your self-esteem, finding the hobbies that you like is really important. Doing hobbies that you are good at is a good way to make sure that you improve your self-esteem.

So, how do you figure out which hobbies you want to do?

The answer to that is…try them all!

If you are not sure yet what kinds of interests you have or you are curious about trying some new hobbies, then it can be helpful to experiment with hobbies in different areas like sports, art, music, cooking and other things that seem interesting to you.

Here are some fun hobbies that you could try:

- ✪ Playing team sports like football, cricket, basketball, hockey and lacrosse.

- ✪ Playing individual sports like tennis, swimming, cycling and golf.

- ✪ Painting, drawing sculpting and other crafts.

- ✪ Chess and other board games.

- ✪ Video games.

- ✪ Creative writing – stories, poems and songwriting.

- ✪ Learning a musical instrument like the piano, guitar, clarinet or violin.

- ✪ Having a pet – but make sure that you ask permission from your mum and dad first.

These are just a few of the hobbies that you can try. You will definitely find one that you really enjoy and it will improve your confidence too. You can also make new friends through your hobbies if you are a part of a club. This is also good for confidence because when people want to spend time with you and you know that they enjoy having you around, it can really boost your self-esteem.

Girls and Relationships

When you get to the age of 11 or 12, and you start to go to high school, you might find that your feelings for girls also start to change. Before, they were just your friends or even those annoying long-haired people that look different to you.

Now, you might have noticed new feelings inside your chest when you look at girls. All of the sudden, they look pretty and they smell good when you are around them. You might want to hold their hands or kiss them. These new urges and feelings are probably going to feel really weird to you at first. When you first have those kinds of emotions, you might feel strange because you have never known them before. Now, when you see a girl and you feel butterflies in your tummy or your face turns hot and red when you are around a girl, that can be very weird to you.

It will still be a few years before you start dating or have a girlfriend but it is good to be aware of the changing feelings that you have as you get older. Girls, just like boys, have these same kinds of feelings. When you see a girl and you think she is pretty or funny or interesting, that might mean that you like her. Many boys can be tempted to try and get a girl's attention by being mean to her. After all, if you are mean to her that will mean that she will remember you, right? Well, no, this is not always the best plan. Yes, she will remember you but she will not remember you for the right reasons.

So, instead of being mean to a girl that you like, it is better to try and find some interests that you share and that can mean that the two of you become good friends. It can be really fun to have friends that are girls. Even though you might like to spend time with other boys, girls can be a lot of fun to be around and they can also give you really good advice when you have a problem.

For some boys, talking to girls can be pretty difficult though. You might find that you do not have the confidence to talk to a girl, especially if you like her. If you are naturally shy, then there are ways to start talking to a girl so that you can be friends with her but it is a good idea to go slowly so that you do not get overwhelmed or scared when you are trying to make a new friend.

- ✪ Say hello to the girl you want to talk to regularly. You do not have to say more than that, at first. Just be friendly and smile at her so that she knows that you are a nice person.

- ✪ Find a good time to talk to the girl. For example, if you are in class and she sits at the desk next to yours, you could ask her a question about something the teacher was talking about. Or, if you see her in the playground, you could ask her if you have homework for a class that you share with her.

✪ Look for things that you both like. Ask her about what she's into. So, she might really be a fan of Disney movies and you might not like those. But she might also really love pop music and you do like that. So, talk about the bands and singers that you like and why you like them.

✪ Understand that some girls are shy too. If you talk to a girl and she does not seem to want to talk to you, that might be because she is shy. It is easy to think that she does not like you – which can cause you to lose confidence. But that might not be true. For a lot of girls, at this age in life, talking to boys can be scary because girls have new feelings that are starting to affect them and they are also confused.

✪ Remember that girls are just people too. When you talk to a girl, there is no more reason to be shy or anxious or embarrassed than when you talk to another boy. Knowing this can be reassuring for you and help you to get over any fears that you have about talking with girls.

Understanding girls

Many adult men will tell you that they do not understand the women in their lives. The same is true for many boys trying to understand girls at your age. Right now, girls of your age are also going through lots of changes in their bodies, their brains and their lives in general. While boys and girls are different in

58

some ways and it can be hard to understand them sometimes, you are both learning to adapt to the new changes that you experience.

Just like boys, girls also go through puberty. However, their bodies and brains change differently from the changes that you are seeing. Knowing more about what girls go through can help you to understand them and learn how to be friends with them. Unlike boys, girls do not have a lot of the hormone testosterone that we talked about earlier in the book. Instead, girls are more affected by a hormone called oestrogen when they go through puberty. This hormone also makes their body change in lots of different and new ways.

Girls will also change in their minds too and start to experience lots of new feelings. Also, they might have some mood swings. You might have noticed that your mum or your older sisters sometimes seem sad or angry for no reason. This is because the hormones in their body affect their feelings. This is just like what you are going through when you feel sad or angry or confused for no reason.

As you get older, girls will be a big part of your life. You will notice that part of the reason that you want to look good and feel confident with your body is to impress them and make them like you. These are natural feelings and during your teenage years, you will notice them a lot more.

If you have questions about girls or the new feelings that you are experiencing, it can be useful and helpful to talk to your mum and dad. They can support you through the changing feelings that you have right now and it can be really nice to be able to be open and honest with them about this.

Finding Role Models

A role model is something that you can look up to and learn from in your life. As a boy and a future man, it is very important to have a good role model in your life. This should be someone who will support you and who you can talk to and ask them for advice. When you are finding it hard to cope with something or you have problems in your life, a role model can be good to look up to for support and help.

For some boys, their role model is their dad, stepdad, older brother, uncle or even a teacher or family friend. But not every boy has this in their life. If you do have a good role model, then it is important that you talk to them about your feelings and ask them for advice when you are unsure about something.

For example, if you are finding a class hard in school, do not just struggle with it on your own. Talk to the person that you can trust and tell them how you are feeling. They will probably be able to help you or find you someone else that can give you extra lessons to help.

Another example of when you might find things difficult is when you first start to feel an attraction to another person. So, if there is a girl in your class whom you think is pretty and you want to talk to her but you are nervous about doing it, talk to your role model and seek their advice on the best way to act.

Sometimes, boys can do silly things around the girls they like. You might not know how to talk to a girl so you are mean to her instead. This can make her dislike you and ruin any chances of her liking you back. Talking to a role model before you act in a silly way can make sure that you do not ruin things.

If you have noticed that you have some problems with the way that you look, a role model can also give you tips and advice on how to make the best of yourself. So, they might tell you that you would look better if you cut your hair or if you wear different types of clothes. Role models or mentors are a really good support system for you to turn to in all kinds of times and situations.

Of course, as you know, not every boy has a male role model in his life. When you do not have a man that you can look up to and learn from him about how to become a man yourself, it can be really hard. You might feel like you are missing out or you might feel sad and lonely. This can make your self-esteem lower because you feel like you do not have the things that you need in your life.

If you do not have an actual person in your life that can be a male role model, there are many famous people who can inspire you. For example, there are many celebrities that offer life advice and tips to boys and this can be helpful. Another option is to turn to a teacher or a coach from a sports team. They can help to guide you through some of the hard and changing years that are ahead of you and give you support when you need it.

While it is important to have men who are your role models, you can also look up to the women in your life as role models. For example, your mum, grandma, auntie, sister or female teachers can teach you a lot of things about life and give you the advice you need. Women sometimes give you a different view on life from men.

Learning Your Identity

Right now, you are in a period of time when a lot of changes are happening around you. We have covered many of those changes in this book such as:

- ✪ Puberty

- ✪ Body changes

- ✪ School changes

- ✪ Changes between old friends and new friends

- ✪ New pressures from school

- ✪ New activities

With all these changes happening, you might be wondering: "Who am I?" In a time of change, sometimes you need to spend some time figuring out more about your identity and what really makes you special.

Everyone goes through times when they feel that their self-esteem is low and they do not have confidence. In this chapter, we are going to look at how you can start to figure out your personal identity and use that to build your confidence. As you get older, that will be really good for making new friends, finding a job and eventually finding a girlfriend and even getting married!

Developing your sense of identity now can help you to feel more stable as you head into the teenage years in front of you. You may already have started thinking about what makes you an individual and how your own talents and personality will affect your life in the future. You will spend the next few years learning about yourself and discovering more about yourself.

It is very important to learn about your identity in a healthy way. This means that you should stay away from bad people who try to influence you to do bad things. We talked about avoiding "peer pressure" earlier in the book as this can affect your life badly. The things you do, the people you meet and the things you achieve can help to make you the boy that you are now and the man that you will become in the future. It is very exciting to learn more about yourself, but it can also be very scary too.

You might notice that over the next few years, you look more at things like your beliefs, your gender, your sexuality and your ethics. If you spend time around good, happy and positive people you are more likely to have positive beliefs and be a happier person in the future.

So, what can you do to understand more about your own identity?

✪ Talk to the people around you and discuss the issues that are on your mind. For example, as you start to become more interested in news and current affairs do not be afraid to ask your mum or dad to explain what is going on to put your mind at rest when you are concerned about something.

✪ Find ways to recover from something sad or upsetting happening. If, for example, you do badly on a test that you studied for really hard, it can upset you a lot. Instead of seeing this as a failure, see it as a way to learn what went wrong and how it could go better the next time.

✪ Listen to the compliments and praise that people give you. Sometimes many boys and girls listen to the bad things that people say and they ignore the good stuff. Try to focus more on the good things because that will make you learn all about the wonderful qualities that you have and will help you to feel happier and more confident as you become a teenager.

✪ Try not to compare yourself to other people. It might be really tempting to compare yourself to other boys but it is important to realise that every boy is an individual. Even if you see a boy who seems to have more money or friends or talents than you do, you do not know what else is going on in his life. He may be happy or he may be unhappy but there is no way to know. Instead, focus on building your own skills and talents and look at all the good things that you have in your own life.

Learning about your identity and who you are on the inside is a really important step to becoming a future man. Appreciate all the good things that you have in life and focus on them instead of any bad things. This will give you a stable start as you continue to see many changes over the next few years.

Body care and self-esteem

Body care and self-esteem are very closely linked to each other. In this part of the book, we are going to look at some of the most important parts of taking care of your changing body and making you feel better about yourself if your self-esteem or confidence is low.

We have already looked at the practical parts of understanding how puberty can affect your body and the various changes that you may go through as well as how you can take care of your body when it comes to making sure that you have good hygiene. There is one other way that you can make sure that you keep your self-esteem high and do not feel bad about things and this is to learn to love yourself.

At first, that might sound very strange to you. We hear a lot that it is bad to love ourselves because it means that we are "stuck up" or "snobbish" but loving your own body and appreciating what you have is really important.

Taking care of your body

As you hit puberty, you will go through many changes in your body, like the ones that we talked about earlier in this book. You are growing hair in places where you didn't use to have hair; your voice is changing and will start to experience erections.

This is why it is even more important to take care of your changing body than ever before because you want to keep yourself in good shape. If you are doing all the right practical things like taking regular exercise, eating healthily and practising good hygiene, you are on the right track. But, even then, you may still look for faults in your body and find things that you think are wrong with yourself, if you do not feel like you are "perfect".

A lot of the time, people think that wanting to look good to others is mostly a "girl thing." But this is not true. As a boy, growing toward becoming a man, you will know that you want people to like the way you look and that you might have some ways that you feel a little insecure.

For many boys, you might have heard things in the media or on television about the "perfect body." The truth is that the perfect body does not exist. If you are feeling anxious or worried about the way that your body looks, it is normal at your age. You might even compare yourself to the way your friends look and that is also normal. However, every single body is different and equally perfect in its own way.

Your body is a wonderful thing. It can do many things. Have you ever really thought about it? Think about it when you are eating. Look at the way all the bones and the muscles are linked to each other. Think about the way that your brain sends messages through millions of tiny little nerves to tell your arm and your hand to pick up the food from your plate and move it to your mouth. This is an incredible thing and if you are finding it hard to really appreciate your body, you can use this tool to understand why it is so great.

For example, when you are walking, focus on your legs and your feet. Look at the way they are made and how they are strong enough to move you forward. Or when you stretch your body in the morning, consider how the muscles move under your skin. All these things are amazing and, even when you feel down, you can see why you should love your body.

Boosting your self-esteem

Are there days when you look in the mirror and you do not feel very good about what you see? Does your hair not look right? Do you have acne starting to show on your face? Do you feel too skinny or too chubby?

The truth is that *everybody feels this way sometimes!*

Whether you are 8, 12, 25 or 50, you may always have parts of your body or face that you do not like or do not feel comfortable with. What we are going to look at now is how to learn to love yourself and feel good about yourself even if there are things that you do not like about yourself.

There are a few tools that you can use to boost your self-esteem and your confidence. These are easy techniques that can work wonders, even though they are so simple. They are good to use whatever you are feeling down about – your image, fights with friends, family conflicts or worries about your schoolwork.

Affirmations: This is a word that means saying good things to yourself and praising yourself, even if you do not feel like it. Have you ever really wanted your favourite sports team or player to win a game even if you knew that they were probably not going to? So, you told your friends that they would *definitely* win even if you didn't believe it at first? Then, the more you told your friends that your team was going to win, the more you believed it too?

Well, *affirmations* or self-praise works in the same way. So, if you believe that you are too skinny, tell yourself that you are perfect. Keep repeating it every morning and every night. **"I am perfect."** If you think that you are not smart enough, repeat to yourself that you *are* smart enough. **"I am smart."**

Your brain is very complicated, like a computer or an electrical plug. It has a type of wiring inside it. When you repeat this praise to yourself, you are changing the way the wires work in your head and create new paths inside your brain. You can make yourself believe the things you say to yourself.

Some good ways to praise yourself are:

✪ **"I am good enough."**

✪ **"I am very smart."**

✪ **"I am handsome."**

✪ **"People like me."**

✪ **"I am good at sports."**

72

Breathing: Breathing is something everyone does but you might not even have thought about it before. You might also not know that you can use your breath you make you feel better and calm yourself down when you feel upset or worried about something.

A really good breathing tool to use is calming breathing that you can do if you feel angry or upset about something. With this, you breathe in slowly through your nose, continuing until you have counted to ten in your head. You breathe out again through your mouth, counting to five beats. Keep repeating this until you find that you feel much calmer and the anger starts to fade a little.

By using calming breathing, it can stop you from doing something silly like shouting at people or even becoming upset with them. So, when you feel like your emotions or your temper are starting to get out of control, try this breathing and see if it can help you to feel better.

Talking to a counsellor: If you feel upset or sad a lot of the time, then it is a good idea to tell your mum, dad or someone else that you can trust. Feeling sad, anxious, worried or stressed is normal for everyone sometimes but if you feel like that *all* of the time and you have no confidence or find it hard to be around other people without getting upset, then there are people that can help you.

There is nothing to be ashamed of if you need to talk to a counsellor. A counsellor is someone who can help you to feel better about yourself by finding out what is making you feel down or stressed. For example, you might have a few worries on your mind, like school, girls, friends or even problems at home.

The great thing about a counsellor is that they will not judge at all. They will listen and understand what you are going through, giving you tips on how to feel better.

The "Embarrassing" Stuff

As you will know by now from reading this book, your body and feelings are going to change a lot over the next few years. This can mean that you will go through some things that might seem embarrassing to you.

One of the biggest changes that you will start to experience are erections. This is where your penis becomes stiff and from around the age of nine or ten, it can happen to boys a lot. Sometimes, it can happen in places or at times when you wish it would not happen, such as in your school classes or when you are playing sports.

You will also notice that you often experience an erection in the mornings when you wake up from sleep. You might also wake up in the morning and notice that you have had something that is called a "wet dream." This is when some semen comes out of your penis while you are sleeping. It is a normal thing that pretty much every boy (and man) goes through at some point in their lives.

It can be strange at first to experience these but they happen because your body is preparing itself for when you get older and you become a man. When men are older, they are able to make babies with women. A woman makes an egg every month and this egg can be turned into a baby by the semen from a man. While you have many years to go before you make a baby, your body will one day be capable of producing the seed that makes up half of a baby.

You might have learned about this in school but for many boys of your age, it can be really embarrassing to think about or talk about. Your parents might also have talked to you about how babies are made. Even though it can be embarrassing, it is also really important to understand it because you might be curious about how human life happens and why you are experiencing these new sensations. Basically, your body is preparing you so that someday in the future you will be ready to make a baby.

Even if you feel shy about talking about this topic, it can help you to understand more if you talk to your mum and dad. They can answer the questions that you have and make you realise that you are not alone in the way that you feel right now.

Another "embarrassing" body worry that many boys have is about their penis. One of the most common questions that boys of your age group ask is: "Is it normal in size and shape?" The answer to this is that penises come in many different shapes, sizes and colours. You might have a lot of worries about that right now and you might feel very self-conscious about it. But remember that it will change as you get older so there is no reason to feel bad about it. As you grow up, you will become more comfortable with your body and it will not seem as embarrassing in the future as it does right now.

The important thing is that you should find trusted people that you can talk to, such as calling a kids' helpline, if you have worries about anything to do with your body. You can also ask your parents to take you to your GP so that you can ask them questions too. Even if you feel shy or embarrassed, it can really help you to feel better and more confident if you can ask the questions that you need to ask them and get personal answers that will make you feel like you are just fine.

Conclusion

Now that you have come to the end of this book, you will have learned many new tips for what it means to grow up and feel great about yourself. You are going through a time of big changes and you are moving away from your boyhood and starting to become a man.

Over the next few years, you will notice many more changes and you will explore your identity even more and learn what it means to be *you*. Over time, you might find that have some harder days and some really great days.

Importantly, you now have the important tools that you can use to keep your self-esteem levels high and, even if you have a hard day or week, you will be able to pick yourself up and move forward without getting too down.

Taking care of your body, learning to respect yourself and understanding what keeps you well in your body and mind is very important. Basically, if you take care of your body, it will take care of you throughout your whole life.

As you continue to grow and change, keep in mind that changes can be a very good thing. They show that your life is moving forward and that you have a lot of exciting experiences still in front of you. The world is at your feet and you can enjoy it and all the benefits that will come your way over the coming years.

Disclaimer

This book contains opinions and ideas of the author and is meant to teach the reader informative and helpful knowledge while due care should be taken by the user in the application of the information provided. The instructions and strategies are possibly not right for every reader and there is no guarantee that they work for everyone. Using this book and implementing the information/recipes therein contained is explicitly your own responsibility and risk. This work with all its contents, does not guarantee correctness, completion, quality or correctness of the provided information. Misinformation or misprints cannot be completely eliminated.

Printed in Great Britain
by Amazon

10380955R00048